Why Do We Suffer

and Where Is God

When We Do?

THE JESUS WAY
—SMALL BOOKS *of* RADICAL FAITH—

Why Do We Suffer

and Where Is God When We Do?

VALERIE G. REMPEL

HERALD
P R E S S

Harrisonburg, Virginia

Herald Press
PO Box 866, Harrisonburg, Virginia 22803
www.HeraldPress.com

Library of Congress Cataloging-in-Publication Data
Names: Rempel, Valerie G., author.
Title: Why do we suffer and where is God when we do? / Valerie G. Rempel.
Description: Harrisonburg, Virginia : Herald Press, 2020. | Series: The
   Jesus way: small books of radical faith | Includes bibliographical
   references.
Identifiers: LCCN 2020000276 (print) | LCCN 2020000277 (ebook) | ISBN
   9781513805672 (paperback) | ISBN 9781513806167 (ebook)
Subjects: LCSH: Suffering--Religious aspects--Christianity. |
   Suffering--Biblical teaching. | Theodicy.
Classification: LCC BT732.7 .R46 2020 (print) | LCC BT732.7 (ebook) | DDC
   231/.8--dc23
LC record available at https://lccn.loc.gov/2020000276
LC ebook record available at https://lccn.loc.gov/2020000277

WHY DO WE SUFFER AND WHERE IS GOD WHEN WE DO?
© 2020 by Herald Press, Harrisonburg, Virginia 22803. 800-245-7894.
All rights reserved.
Library of Congress Control Number: 2020000276
International Standard Book Number: 978-1-5138-0567-2 (paperback);
    978-1-5138-0616-7 (ebook)
Printed in United States of America
Cover and interior design by Reuben Graham

Unless otherwise noted, Scripture text is quoted, with permission, from the
New Revised Standard Version, © 1989, Division of Christian Education of the
National Council of Churches of Christ in the United States of America.

Scripture quotations marked (KJV) are taken from the *King James Version* of
the Bible.

24 23 22 21 20   10 9 8 7 6 5 4 3 2 1

Contents

Introduction to The Jesus Way Series from Herald Press

The Jesus Way is good news for all people, of all times, in all places. Jesus Christ "is before all things, and in him all things hold together"; "in him all the fullness of God was pleased to dwell" (Colossians 1:17, 19). The Jesus Way happens when God's will is done on earth as it is in heaven.

But what does it mean to walk the Jesus Way? How can we who claim the name of Christ reflect the image of God in the twenty-first century? What does it mean to live out and proclaim the good news of reconciliation in Christ?

The Jesus Way: Small Books of Radical Faith offers concise, practical theology that helps readers encounter big questions about God's work in the world. Grounded in a Christ-centered reading of Scripture and a commitment to reconciliation, the series aims to enliven the service and embolden the witness of people who follow Jesus. The volumes in the series are written by a diverse community of internationally renowned pastors, scholars, and practitioners committed to the way of Jesus.

The Jesus Way series is rooted in Anabaptism, a Christian tradition that prioritizes following Jesus, loving enemies, and creating faithful communities. During the Protestant Reformation of the 1500s, early Anabaptists who began meeting for worship emphasized discipleship in addition to belief, baptized adults instead of infants, and pledged their allegiance to God over loyalty to the state. Early Anabaptists were martyred for their radical faith, and they went to their deaths without violently resisting their accusers.

Today more than two million Anabaptist Christians worship in more than one hundred countries around the globe. They include Mennonites, Amish, Brethren in Christ, and Hutterites. Many other Christians committed to Anabaptist beliefs and practices remain in church communities in other traditions.

Following Jesus means turning from sin, renouncing violence, seeking justice, believing in the reconciling power of God, and living in the power of the Holy Spirit. The Jesus Way liberates us from conformity to the world and heals broken places. It shines light on evil and restores all things.

Join Christ-followers around the world as we seek the Jesus Way.

Introduction

It was, to paraphrase Alexander of children's book fame, a terrible, horrible, no good, very bad year.[1] A high school friend died of cancer and another landed in the hospital with what turned out to be metastatic breast cancer. She would die the following year. A much-loved aunt succumbed to the ravages of Parkinson's disease and died during the Christmas season. We postponed her funeral so another aunt could have surgery for her recently diagnosed cancer. My workplace was in turmoil and a friend was so angry at me that, for a short season, we could not celebrate the Lord's Supper together. And one fall day, I received a phone call from my father telling me that he was in the hospital being diagnosed with lung cancer. And here you should imagine my stepmother's voice in the background saying, "Don't forget to tell her happy birthday."

Suffering, of course, comes in many forms. I listed a series of personal griefs that were made more sorrowful because I had survived cancer only to lose my mother to that disease a few years later. Perhaps you or someone you love is dealing with another kind of physical or mental health issue. Perhaps you have or are experiencing the pain of infertility, or the loss of a loved one through death or broken relationship. Perhaps you are caring for someone who is suffering and are finding it hard to know how to offer comfort. Perhaps you simply don't know how to make sense of the news, which is so often filled with stories of senseless tragedy.

If you have picked up this book, you probably have your own version of a difficult season of life. Perhaps you are still in the midst of it and are asking the question that is at the heart of this small book: Why do we suffer, and where is God when we do? If so, I hope you will find some helpful ways to think about this question and, ultimately, affirm faith in the God who sustains us even in the midst of our darkest days. I hope this little book will help you think more "Christianly" about these matters. I do believe that God is with us even and especially in the midst of our suffering and sorrow.

1

Why Does Suffering Exist?

There are days when everything seems too much. Between the daily news and our own sorrows, we are tempted to either pull the bedcovers up over our heads or simply collapse, wailing until we are exhausted. The questions rise from the depths. How could this happen? How can we bear another sorrow? Why won't God answer our prayers for relief? Enough is enough, already!

In the face of a suffering world or when overwhelmed by personal pain or grief, we ask what must be one of the most frequently asked questions for people of faith: If an all-powerful and loving God exists, why is there so much suffering in the world?

This is a book about suffering. It seeks to guide readers in exploring the questions we have when faced with pain and suffering—our own, and that of others. Thinking about these questions is essential work for people of faith because the problem of suffering, and of evil itself, is one that confronts us all. When it does, we often struggle to reconcile our belief in the goodness of God with what seems like such pointless and unnecessary suffering. The technical term for exploring these questions is **theodicy**. (Key terms appear in bold and are defined in the glossary.) Theodicy is the attempt to answer the questions that arise when we think about God in relationship to human suffering.

SUFFERING AS A BARRIER TO FAITH

If we are honest, we also recognize that the problem of pain and suffering in our world can act as a barrier to faith. We proclaim that God cares for creation and for the humans made in God's image. We affirm the goodness of God, and God's power. If these things are true, we may begin to wonder why a good and powerful God would allow this level of human suffering. We are left wondering whether God really knows and understands our suffering, and whether or not God is truly good. And deep in our own being, we may begin to wonder if we believe in God at all. Maybe we have made the whole thing up and we would be better off not believing.

SEARCHING FOR MEANING

We ask these kinds of questions because people are meaning-making creatures. We like order and things that make sense to us. We want to believe that everything happens for a reason. When something unexpected happens, we try very hard to make sense of it, to find the reason for what happened. We simply find events easier to accept if we understand, or think we understand, what happened.

If you've ever listened to or been part of a group that learns of some difficult event, say a car accident that left someone hurt or even dead, you have likely heard some version of the following. "Were they driving too fast?" we want to know. "Were the road conditions unsafe?" Perhaps they were texting while driving; everyone knows that is dangerous. We want a reason that isn't simply related to chance, something that will reassure us the next time we are driving that it won't happen to us, because we don't drive too fast (really?), use our phones in the car (never), or set out in bad weather. Unexplained accidents make us feel vulnerable because we fear they could happen to us too. We desperately want to feel safe.

Of course, we try to make sense of good things too. If I receive a promotion at work, it must be because someone has seen me working hard and decided to reward me. If my children are well-behaved, it must be because I am following good child-rearing principles. We might not say it out loud, but a part of us wants to believe that good things really do happen to good people and that bad things happen mostly to bad people.

Except we know that isn't true. Sometimes "good" people suffer horrific loss and "bad" people get away with their misdeeds. It doesn't seem fair, and like the psalmist, we may ask why the wicked prosper (Psalm 73:3). We see that the rain falls on the just and unjust, and that the tornado strikes the houses of both believers and nonbelievers. We want to affirm that God loves and cares for all of creation, but we struggle to understand this mystery of human experience.

UNDERSTANDING OUR TERMS

Let's begin by thinking about what we mean by pain and suffering. Not all pain is bad. Our bodies are designed to register pain as a warning against injury or the presence of illness. The intricacy of sensory receptors sending messages to our brains via nerve fibers serves an important function. The heat we feel as our hands get close to fire or a hot stove reminds us not to touch those sources of danger, while the pain of a sprained ankle keeps us from putting too much weight on the joint and ligaments so they can heal. The ache of tired muscles after hard work or exercise may even feel quite satisfying. On the other hand, severe pain may serve as a warning that something in our body needs attending to, and so we schedule a health appointment. Unless the pain is chronic or debilitating, most of us accept a measure of physical pain as part of the way bodies are designed to function. In this sense, physical pain can be good. We want our bodies to feel!

We also feel emotional pain. Here, too, we accept some pain as reasonable, even good. If we suffer guilt over a misspoken word or some action that has harmed others, we may seek to repair the damage done to a relationship and to mend that which was broken. We may gladly feel the pain that comes from empathy, finding solidarity in shared human experiences that bind people together. Who of us would give up the "pain" that comes from loving a spouse, a parent, a sibling, or a child and being loved in return?

Other kinds of emotional pain can help us learn to thrive. It may hurt for a moment, but learning to accept criticism in school or on the job, or even the disappointment of losing a hard-fought game as part of a sports team, may contribute to our growth. We learn to face obstacles, discover the strength to try again, begin to take pleasure in the game even when we don't win. While these experiences "hurt" for a season or while we may "suffer" the loss, we recognize their usefulness.

Still, we know that emotional pain, like physical pain, can be debilitating. When losing a job puts a family's well-being in jeopardy, we would gladly give up a lesson in resiliency for the security of a steady income. Suffering guilt over a misdeed is quite different from suffering a lifetime of shame for some perceived inadequacy. Suffering chronic mental illness is no more desirable than suffering from any other disease. Watching and suffering alongside a loved one dealing with a terminal illness, an addiction, or some physical or mental limitation that restricts living a full life can be anguishing.

The examples above reflect common, day-to-day experiences. They seem mostly familiar. But human suffering also happens on an enormous scale. For example, in addition to two world wars during the last century, there were horrific acts of genocide. At least six million Jews were put to death during the Holocaust. Those deaths were preceded by some one million Armenians killed at the end of the Ottoman Empire and followed by the more recent Rwandan genocide that left some eight hundred thousand people dead. A brief dig into history provides a much longer list of places and people groups who have suffered around the globe. From the more than twelve million Africans taken into slavery between the sixteenth and nineteenth centuries to the estimated seventy-five to two hundred million people affected by the plague in the fourteenth century, the list goes on and on.

THE IMPACT OF TECHNOLOGY

In an earlier era, people tended to know about what was happening only in their own communities. Travel and communication were limited. In our own day, we are no longer unaware of the effects of slavery, human trafficking, and the destruction caused by war and natural disasters. The daily cycle of news offers a steady diet of violence and hurt, even when it happens in communities far from our own. There are countless examples of pain and loss that exist on an almost unimaginable scale. When we think about these things, it is easy to be overwhelmed, and that becomes its own kind of suffering too.

Part of why we feel so overwhelmed by the scale of suffering is that our awareness of events has grown with advances in technology. Not only do we hear about the latest school shooting or outbreak of violence in some distant part of the world, but we see the pictures and we hear the cries. Our hearts break to see children starving, families removed from their homes, people treated like cattle. Our news media sources continually present stories that break our hearts. Where is God? Doesn't God care?

In exploring our ideas about suffering and God, we quickly come to realize that it isn't so much the presence of pain that distresses us as the degree to which it exists and to which we suffer. Perhaps we can admit that some pain is useful, but how can it be God's will for people to suffer in such meaningless ways? We begin to wonder if God is really in control of the created world.

SIN AND EVIL

For Christians, the search for answers must lead to Scripture. "In the beginning," says the writer of Genesis, "the earth was a formless void and darkness covered the face of the deep" (Genesis 1:1-2). In rich, evocative language, the text continues with an account of the creator God fashioning a world that God declares "good." Sun and moon, day and night, trees and vegetation, water and land creatures, and finally the human beings, male and female, made in the image of God. And all of it declared "good" by its Creator.

This first account of creation is followed by a second story of creation that focuses especially on the human element in the story. In it, the writer depicts God's concern for relationship. It isn't good to be alone, so Adam is united with Eve. They are charged with care for the garden that God has given them, are encouraged to flourish, begin a family, and walk alongside their Creator. They are trusted and given responsibilities, along with just one restriction. They are not to eat or even touch the fruit of one special tree.

If you have read or heard this story from the book of Genesis, you know how this is going to end. The fruit is hard to resist. Even more difficult is resisting the voice of the serpent who pokes and prods until Eve picks the fruit and shares it with Adam. Sin and evil enter the world.

The Bible doesn't say where it comes from or even why it exists, but sin has entered and begun its work of corruption. Adam and Eve experience the first guilty consciences, suffering because they know they have disobeyed a loving God. They try to hide from God, and when discovered, they turn on each other. Eve blames the tricky serpent and Adam blames Eve. No one wants to take responsibility for their own choice to disobey.

Adam and Eve have gained new knowledge, but it comes with a price. There are consequences to their decisions, and they are expelled from the garden. There will be pain in childbirth and conflict in relationships, and the ground will resist easy harvest. What God created with such care has been thoroughly disrupted.

THE CONSEQUENCES OF SIN

Why should Adam and Eve's failure to obey God have such lasting consequences? Christian thinkers have wrestled long and hard with how and why this first sin is passed down to all subsequent generations. The early church leader Augustine offered three analogies that continue to shape our understanding.[1] The first analogy is to view sin as a kind of hereditary disease that is passed down through the generations. In this way of thinking, Adam and Eve passed along a kind of predisposition to sin that continues to be seen in each generation. The second way is to see sin as a power that holds people captive. It is so strong that we cannot break free by ourselves. The third way is simply to see sin in terms of guilt that is passed down through the generations.

Each of these ways offers us a glimpse into sin's destructive force. Whether we view sin as a kind of weakness in humanity or as a power that holds us, we recognize the reality of sin and the way it hurts people. What continues to be important is to see this as a result of human choice so that we don't blame God for what might look like a weakness in the creation of humanity. At its most simple, we can see the first humans' decision as a forerunner of our own, for we, too, resist the good and disobey God. We, too, experience the effects of sin and are prone to evil.

SIN BREAKS RELATIONSHIPS

One helpful way to understand the aftereffects of the fall is to see how it breaks relationships.[2] First and foremost is the break between God and humanity. Adam and Eve try to hide, knowing they have disappointed the one they knew as divine friend. This is followed by the break in relationship between the humans themselves, so much so that Adam and Eve's children fight amongst themselves and one brother kills another. There is a break between humanity and the natural world: people struggle to control nature but are also subject to it.

People even experience this corruption in their own beings: bodies and minds don't always function in healthy ways. To put it simply, things don't work as they were designed to work!

The biblical account of creation and of this break in relationship offers us a way to understand the reality of our world and our experiences. To say that things don't work as they were designed to work and that we are subject to that disruption is a way to describe the effects of sin and the evil that people commit. Our bodies hurt and experience illness. Genes sometimes mutate in disastrous ways. Viruses gain strength and travel the globe. Like Adam and Eve's own children, we turn on each other and seek to cause harm. Political and economic forces work for both good and ill, so sometimes they oppress and even harm people. There is pain and evil, and we suffer.

2

How Can I Believe in a God Who Allows So Much Suffering?

In a cartoon published shortly after the terrorist attacks on the East Coast, including New York City, in September 2001, a cartoonist referred to the question in our chapter heading as one of the top FAQs about God.[1] FAQ has become the acronym for "frequently asked questions," and in the wake of disasters, natural or human-made, people may begin to wonder whether it is possible or even right to believe in God. After all, if God is not all-powerful and in control of the world and its events, why should we believe?

Our ideas about God's power, presence, and activity in the world are shaped by the Bible, but also by human thought about the idea of a divine being. The Bible describes God as creator and ascribes miracles to God. God is described as everlasting, as holy and righteous, as just and mighty. God is the one who knows our hearts, sees our actions, and, at times, intervenes on behalf of God's people. Through these descriptions of God, we have come to think about God as something very different from ourselves. God is beyond our capacity to understand, yet is in relationship with people.

In whatever ways we think about God, it is clear that God is unlike any other created being. "To whom then will you liken God," asks the prophet in Isaiah 40:18, "or what likeness compare with him?" While the Bible tells us that we are made in the image of God, God is not made in the image of humankind. Because of that, we often struggle to understand God and God's relationship with humanity.

GOD'S ACTIVITY IN THE WORLD

There are many stories in the Bible of God's activity in the affairs of humankind. Because of these examples, Christians can often be heard saying that "God is in control." It is important for us to consider what we mean by this kind of statement and how our ideas about "control" relate to our understanding of God's power and authority.

As Christians, we believe that God not only created the world but remains active in it. We affirm that God holds things together, thus sustaining the world we inhabit. This isn't to suggest that Christians don't believe in science or the physical ways we have come to understand how the world works. It is simply to confess that there is divine intention and activity in this world and to acknowledge that what exists has not come into being by accident.

What kind of presence and activity does God have? There are many ways to think about that.[2]

Some people have suggested that God simply created the world and the natural laws that govern it but now leaves it alone to keep running as if it were some kind of self-winding watch. This view was especially popular in the seventeenth and eighteenth centuries and is referred to as **deism**. From this perspective, God may care about the world, but it is designed to function on its own. In this way of thinking, God is a bit like an absentee landlord who owns the property but leaves the upkeep to the occupants. When things go wrong, well, they simply go wrong. It isn't God's fault, nor can we expect God to intervene.

By contrast, many Christians throughout history have insisted that God has ultimate control over all that happens because God is king, or sovereign, over all things. Kingship is language that the Bible uses to describe God's power and especially God's authority. It is one among many metaphors used to help us understand who God is and how we should relate to God. To be a ruling monarch is to have great power and to exert one's will or authority. Kings order things to happen. They demand ultimate loyalty from their subjects. Of course, kings are also charged with the welfare of their people. Good kings seek the well-being of their subjects. They uphold justice and, if needed, punish wrongdoing. You can easily see how what we know of human kings might shape the way we view God and God's activity in the world.

Another way of thinking about God's activity in the world comes from the writings of Thomas Aquinas, a theologian living in the thirteenth century. **Thomism** suggests that God is not directly in control of events, especially those we experience as harmful or evil, but is working through secondary causes. For example, if humans build a dam on a beautiful flowing river, but that dam is weak and breaks, the resulting flood is the result of a secondary cause. It isn't the fault of the first cause, God's creation of the river, but rather the second cause, the dam that broke and caused the flooding.

Yet another perspective is a more recent twentieth-century development related to **process thought**. From this perspective, God is at work through the unfolding of events that are not predetermined. God's primary way of working is through influence or persuasion. You might think of God's activity as a kind of divine nudge, encouraging humanity in the right direction, although people are always free to accept or reject the persuasive force of the divine. This is very different from the kingship model above, and many Christians are troubled by what seems to be a lack of foreknowledge and even divine power in this way of thinking.

Some people of faith insist that God isn't in direct control of all that happens. They find it easier to understand God's actions as a response to human choices and the natural workings of our world. In this way of thinking, God is interacting with the world and all that is in it in a dynamic fashion. We might think of it as a kind of partnership with humanity. God is clearly present and active but is not so highly directive, not "in control" in the way I have used the term above. This view is sometimes referred to as the **openness of God**.

Some Christians believe that the openness model takes the presence and power of sin and evil more seriously in that God is actively engaged with the powers and principalities that are described in the Bible. From this perspective, God's "control" is affirmed in a confidence that God will ultimately win and that God's plan for the redemption of the world will come to pass. God's knowledge is affirmed in God's ability to know and respond to all that is possible and all that happens rather than in knowing precisely what will happen at any given time.

This perspective tends to focus more on how God is with people in their suffering and less on how God might be directing events that cause suffering.

As you can see from the above, Christians vary in their understanding of how God relates to our world and how much God influences events. At one end of the spectrum are those who argue that everything that happens, happens because God wills it, while at the other end are those who see God as disengaged or at least not directly responsible for what happens in our world. Each perspective offers its own challenges as we think about the presence of evil in our world.

WRESTLING WITH "CONTROL"

A student I knew was trying to understand why God had wrecked his car. He had been on the way to deliver it to a prospective buyer when an accident happened, and the sale fell through. My student was certain there was a reason for what had happened, other than inattentive driving! He seemed sure that God had willed the accident, but he was having trouble understanding what God's purpose was in stopping the sale of the vehicle. There was no immediate or obvious reason or "good" for the car to be wrecked. On the contrary, he lost a sale and the buyer lost a good vehicle. Still, my student was certain that God had intended the accident as part of some plan or will on God's part and kept trying to puzzle it out.

It is possible that the accident didn't happen by chance and that in causing or even allowing the accident God was working toward some larger aim. Just because we don't understand something doesn't mean God isn't present or acting. At the same time, if we take the presence of sin and evil seriously, especially their corrupting influence in our world, perhaps accidents are just that, accidents.

Of course, some people find it far more acceptable and certainly more comforting to believe that God willed an event than to simply think that something happened by accident. For them, God's power is diminished and God's knowledge is threatened if that power or knowledge is limited in some way. For many people, it is easier to accept something that is disappointing or "bad" if they can believe that what has happened is in God's will. We want to believe in order, not chaos.

While living with the mystery of God's action in the kind of everyday accident that I've described seems reasonable, there are problems with seeing everything that happens as directed by God. For example, I might believe that God has sent me a physical ailment as a way to strengthen my trust in God or teach some needed lesson. That may help me accept something that causes me and those who love me to suffer. I may find meaning in what is happening if I believe that God has sent illness my way for a specific reason. Perhaps my character is being shaped for the good by the experience in ways that draw me closer to God. Maybe I needed to learn patience or to trust in God more fully. Maybe the people who care for me need to be encouraged in their faith or prompted to become better caregivers.

But what about others who suffer debilitating illness or some harm that comes as a result of evil? There are children who are abandoned or abused by their parents or other adults around them. Slavery and human trafficking continue to be problems in our world. Surely God does not will the devastation caused by rape or other abuses in order for victims to learn some lesson; it seems unlikely that their character will be shaped for the better by experiencing such devastating harm. Few Christians would suggest that God is directing the incidents of terror and violence that occur with such frequency in our world or that God wills such harm to vulnerable people.

Of course, just because a reason isn't immediately evident to us, or because we experience something as an example of evil, doesn't mean there isn't some divine action or purpose involved. Even people who insist that God is in immediate control of all that happens might point to the need to trust that these events are working toward a larger goal, even if that remains beyond our knowledge or ability to comprehend.

For example, some might argue that what we experience as evil is really evidence of divine punishment or judgment for sin. We'll explore that idea further later on. Others might argue that we shouldn't question God's actions but simply accept them. They rightly point to the mystery of God and that we can't know all of what God intends. They argue that we simply need to accept what happens, submitting ourselves to God's will for our lives.

For other Christians, however, a too direct understanding of God's "control" doesn't offer enough room for the free choices that people make. They worry that too narrow a description of God's control ends up with a view of God that is more like a puppet master pulling the strings of the creatures on a stage. The puppets are entertaining and might look as if they are choosing their actions, but in reality, they are being directed by unseen hands. Even more troubling, they see this understanding of the idea of God's "control" as making God somehow responsible for the evil that people commit. After all, if God is directly "in control" of all things, then God must somehow be "in control" of what we experience as evil.

TAKING CARE IN THE LANGUAGE WE USE

As followers of Jesus, we need to be careful about how we speak of these things and the way we describe God to ourselves and to others. And we need to take seriously the effects of sin and evil. If, as the Bible suggests, sin has entered the world and corrupted it, then it may be more helpful to see pain and suffering as a consequence of that activity rather than as something directed by God. The effects of sin and evil become a problem for us that God is fully capable of solving. Evil isn't directed by a loving God; rather, it is something God opposes. Furthermore, God is infinitely capable and can be trusted to do all that God has promised.

If we take seriously the idea of sin's corrupting influence on our world, then we also need to accept our vulnerability to that influence. Bad things do happen to people, even people who have put their trust in God. Bodies are still subject to illness, pain, and death. Accidents happen, and people and things are harmed. Sometimes we are in the path of destructive forces, whether those are natural forces or events directed by human will. Indeed, the Bible describes Satan as a roaring lion, prowling around seeking someone to devour (1 Peter 5:8). If God is truly with us, then we can face the possibility of such events with confidence that God will be at work.

Thinking about the ongoing influence of sin in our world also encourages us to take seriously what the Bible calls "principalities and powers." This is language used in the New Testament book of Ephesians and can be understood as the forces that oppress people, the unjust systems and ways the world works to privilege the strong and take advantage of the weak (Ephesians 6:12 KJV). The Bible also describes these as demonic forces, and in that description, it is clear that they exist in opposition to God. Some people use the language of

spiritual warfare to describe the way these forces oppose God and oppress people.

It is important to remember that as followers of Jesus, we believe that in Jesus, God has begun the work of ending the effects of sin. In Jesus' death and resurrection, we are promised an ultimate end to suffering and the effects of sin and death in our world. The Bible teaches us that in raising Jesus from the dead, God has demonstrated the power to ultimately win over the forces of sin and evil. This is our Christian hope: that God will redeem the entire cosmos and restore all things to right relationship with God.

GOD'S SELF-LIMITATION

One helpful way of understanding God's power and control is to consider the limits that God appears to have imposed on God's own activity in the world and especially in relationship to humankind. If we believe that God created people with the ability to obey or disobey God, then we must take seriously the choices people make and the resulting consequences. By God's own choosing, these decisions may limit God's own actions.

Imagine, for example, that you are a teacher offering a group of children a choice between two activities. After much consultation and negotiation, the children arrive at option A as their choice. Assuming that you will do only one activity as promised, at this point, option B is no longer a possibility, unless you override their choice. Their decision, together with your earlier decision as their teacher, has limited what can now happen.

Of course, in real life, we know that sometimes we can choose more than one option or run them sequentially so that we get some form of both A and B. Perhaps I start my professional life as a teacher, but that doesn't mean I can't go into business later. Some choices don't limit the possibility of others, while some decisions really are irrevocable. If I choose to stay home with a book on a Sunday morning and watch the clock tick past the time for the worship service, attending church is soon no longer an option. At least, not on this Sunday and not at my regular place of worship. I can't go back in time and reverse that decision.

This analogy can be helpful in thinking about God's power and presence in the world. If God created humankind with the freedom to make choices, even sinful ones, then God has essentially limited "control" by sharing it to some degree with others.

You might be thinking that this makes sense, but that surely God could override human decisions. Yes, although that sets up another kind of problem.

Let's go back to the example of a teacher with a classroom of children. If, as the teacher, you meant for the group to engage in option B all along, and even after the children choose option A you insist on following your own decision, then offering the children a choice was a kind of lie or even an attempt to deceive them into thinking they could choose. You were in charge all along.

It is important to remember that one of our primary claims about the character of God is that God is trustworthy. The Bible repeatedly tells us that God is not like humans, who can go back on their word, or who practice deception. God's own holy character prevents God from sinning or engaging in evil. This is good news! We can trust God to keep the promises God has made.

The point is that in choosing some actions, we rule out the possibility of others. In this way, we might understand God's activity in the world to be "limited" by God's decision to relate to humanity in a way that allows humans the freedom to make decisions. God's own actions may also be thought to be "limited" by God's own steadfastly holy character.

I'm fairly certain that an astute reader will be able to offer an example that might seem to contradict God's unwillingness to override human choices. For example, a parent might allow a toddler to choose the direction she runs but will quickly swoop her up if she seems to be in danger of hurting herself. We establish all kinds of rules and laws to govern people's behavior in an effort to make them choose what we want them to do. If God is the divine parent, then surely a loving God can be trusted to intervene when we are in danger, or to nudge us in the direction we ought to go.

Yes, we do look to God's Spirit to guide us, and we do pray for wisdom in our decision-making. As followers of Jesus, we seek to lead holy lives and to resist the sinful practices that harm others and ourselves. We also know that throughout history, people have given witness to events that seem clearly directed by God. We do, after all, look for God to be active and engaged in the world. Still, the effects of sin are present in our world and we, too, suffer. Believing in God doesn't function as a kind of insurance policy against difficult human experiences.

GOD SUFFERS WITH US

In limiting God's own self, God may also suffer out of love for creation and for humankind. Like parents grieving a poor choice their child makes, a choice that will lead to some degree of suffering, God surely suffers with us. It seems inconceivable that a loving God could remain untouched by the weight of human suffering or the groanings of the earth.

Sin and its consequences are a problem in need of a solution. As followers of Jesus, we believe that in Jesus, God has begun the work of addressing human pain and suffering. In the **incarnation**, God took on human form, becoming like us in all things except for sin. In this, we can be assured that God fully understands what it is to be human, to suffer loss and even death.

God knows what it is to suffer. As God the Father, God watched God's own Son suffer the indignities and physical pain of the crucifixion. As the Son, Jesus Christ, God suffered death itself. Although God has not chosen to prevent all human suffering, we can be assured that God understands what it is that we experience and will be with us in our suffering.

3

Do I Suffer Because I've Been Bad, or Will It Make Me Good?

If you have ever had something bad happen to you, you may have been on the receiving end of well-intentioned people trying to help you make sense of what occurred. In a season of illness many years ago, I received a card assuring me that my sickness had brought a group of people together to pray for me. I remember thinking that it was nice that people were forming a meaningful Christian community, but I wasn't sure my illness and the suffering I was experiencing were worth that, at least not to me!

As has been noted several times in the previous chapters, people long to make sense of what is happening in their lives, and we look for good in the midst of suffering. This can be positive, as it pushes us to search for where God is present and active in our experiences. As Christians, we believe that, as Scripture says, "all things work together for good for those who love God, who are called according to his purpose" (Romans 8:28). At the same time, we need to be careful that we don't confuse evil with good. God's power and willingness to transform what happens "for God's purposes," shouldn't cause us to dismiss pain and suffering by treating them as good in and of themselves.

CAN GOOD COME FROM EVIL?

One familiar story from the Bible that helps us understand God's power to bring good out of something bad occurs in the book of Genesis. Starting in chapter 37, we read the story of Joseph and his many brothers, all sons of a man named Jacob. Joseph was a favorite of his father, what we might call the spoiled baby of the family. One day while the brothers were out tending their animals, Joseph's father sent him to check on his brothers. His brothers, tired of the way their father favored Joseph, saw this as an opportunity to get rid of him. They threw him into a pit and, when a group of travelers came along, sold him into slavery.

Joseph ended up in Egypt, eventually becoming a trusted administrator under the pharaoh. Although he began as a slave, his skills were found useful, and he gradually became a valued member of the court. Many years later, during an extended time of famine, Joseph was surprised to meet his brothers who had traveled to Egypt to find food. Of course, they didn't recognize Joseph. There was no reason to think their little brother was now a powerful person in Egypt.

As the story unfolds, we learn that Joseph was able to help save his brothers and their extended households, even reuniting with his beloved father before Jacob died. Forgiving his brothers for their treachery, Joseph said, "Even though you intended to do harm to me, God intended it for good, in order to preserve a numerous people, as he is doing today" (Genesis 50:20).

Some people read this story, and especially Joseph's statement about God meaning his brothers' actions for "good," as evidence that God directed the difficult experiences in Joseph's life so he would be in Egypt to save his brothers. It seems more in keeping with God's holy character, however, to see the good that came out of this experience as evidence of God's power to transform what was meant for evil into something that served to bring about God's intentions for the well-being of Jacob's family. God doesn't need evil in order to accomplish God's will!

It is reassuring to see how God was present and at work within actions that were meant for harm. For example, we see the travelers who bought Joseph from his brothers as apparently sent by God to rescue him from being killed and to save his brothers from the act of murder. Certainly, the writer of Genesis understood God to be using this situation to save Jacob's family. The Bible frequently gives witness to God's desire and intention for good, and in the overall story of the Bible, this becomes one of many events in the forming of God's people, Israel.

The fact that God brought good out of something so difficult offers us hope and may prompt us to look for the good that may come out of our own suffering. We must be careful, however, not to become blind to the reality of suffering or to dismiss our own or others' suffering as sent by God for some necessary purpose in the world. Being betrayed by family members and sold into slavery isn't "good." Joseph's suffering was real. Joseph was enslaved, and at one point was even unjustly thrown into prison. The fact that the Bible tells us that God used what happened to save Joseph's family shouldn't blind us to the wrong that was done to him by his own brothers. They truly meant to hurt him.

We shouldn't ever call evil "good" or justify it as somehow meant by God for good. The suffering in our world is all too real, and unlike Joseph in the biblical story, people who suffer may never see how their suffering has brought about any good. The person serving an extended prison sentence may only become bitter and despairing. Suffering a terminal illness may only result in what seems like untimely death. The young widow or widower who loses a spouse may find a new partner and once again experience the richness of a good marriage, but such a person is unlikely to see the pain of that first loss as worth it in order to find joy in a second marriage. This person is unlikely to say, "God took my first spouse in order to give me this new one!"

We must always be careful not to overly interpret people's suffering for them. It is right to believe that God can and will bring about good despite horrific tragedy. That "good" doesn't justify the evil that was done or the suffering that resulted from some act of nature or human will. God doesn't "need" pain and suffering to accomplish God's ends. Indeed, our confession is that God is more than capable of transforming these things and even now is at work for the redemption of the world.

SIN AND EVIL AS INTRUDERS

The Bible describes sin and evil as intruders into God's good creation, not as God's plan or desire for humankind. Any good that comes out of suffering is evidence of God's love and transforming power, and we should rightly be grateful for those things. We should also remember, however, that God's love and transforming power can be rejected. Good doesn't always come out of tragedy, and sometimes tragedy multiplies in ways that increase suffering. This, too, is a sign of sin's corruption and a reminder that the kingdom of God is not yet fully present.

The New Testament gives us another story that can be helpful in thinking about the causes of suffering. In John 9 we follow along with the disciples as they walk with Jesus and encounter a man who had been blind from birth. The conversation reveals something about the disciples' assumptions. "Who sinned," they ask, "this man or his parents?" They seem to view this man's blindness as punishment for someone's misdeeds.

It is true that suffering may come about because of sin. Sometimes there are consequences to our actions that result in loss or other kinds of pain. In the Bible, we read that Adam and Eve were expelled from the garden, and we see evidence of their suffering and the effects of their sin in the stories that follow. We could name any number of examples of suffering that come about because of what we would call sin. For example, we know that unfaithfulness to a spouse may lead to a break in the relationship that permanently disrupts a family's life, leading to separation and divorce. Malicious pranks may result in physical harm to others, causing a lifetime of disability or even ending a life. Sin and evil have consequences. We should take them seriously.

We need to be careful, however, in assuming that illness or other kinds of suffering are directly related to someone's particular sin. It is one thing to see and take seriously the overarching narrative of sin's influence in the world. It is another to interpret a specific illness or catastrophe as God's punishment for a specific sinful action. How can we know that?

In the story of the man born blind, for example, Jesus tells the disciples that no one sinned. "Neither this man nor his parents sinned," Jesus says; "he was born blind so that God's works might be revealed in him" (John 9:3). Like the story of Joseph and his brothers, the Bible suggests that what has happened offered an opportunity for God to be at work, for God to be glorified. Jesus' healing action in his encounter with the man gave the disciples evidence of God's power to heal and God's compassion for those who suffer.

Some Christians might read this story as evidence that God caused the man's blindness in order to heal him and offer an object lesson to the disciples. It is more helpful, I think, to read this story as one of many healing stories in the gospel accounts of Jesus' life and ministry on earth in which Jesus' actions pointed to his own divine nature and oneness with God the Father. They provided the disciples, and now provide us, with evidence of God's power to redeem and renew creation. They offer us hope that one day, all things will be made right. In the meantime, we continue to live with the effects of our own sin and that of others.

WHAT AM I MEANT TO LEARN?

Some people believe that pain or suffering are sent by God to teach us a lesson. This is a version of the popular saying "Everything happens for a reason," which tends to focus on trying to understand what God wants us to learn. As a child, my father once punished me for misbehaving at the dinner table. When he thought I was sufficiently repentant, he asked me if I was ready to be good. Foolishly, I said no. You won't be surprised to learn that the punishment was extended for an additional period. Clearly, I had not learned my lesson, and my "suffering" continued!

Sometimes we act as if we could put an end to the pain or suffering we are experiencing if we could just figure out what God is trying to teach us. We search our hearts. Is there unconfessed sin? Do I need to become more patient? Maybe I haven't been trusting God enough. Perhaps I need to pray more earnestly or read my Bible more faithfully. We could list all sorts of possible lessons, and they might all be good for us to learn. I suspect, however, that this is far too simple a way to think about pain and suffering. Experiences that result in suffering are not some kind of divine homework that just needs to be completed as quickly as possible so we can pass the "test" and get on with our lives.

It may be more helpful to see any lesson learned through the experience of suffering as part of how God is at work in our experiences. Do we draw closer to God or resist God? Do we look to God for help and to sustain us in loss? Do we seek God's comfort in our grief? Our experiences regularly provide us opportunity to look to God and to have our character shaped by our encounter with God. We can become more Christlike as we endure suffering, or we can abandon our faith altogether. Here, too, God has given us choices.

The point is, there may not be a particular lesson to be learned from suffering, and we can seldom shortcut our pain by seeking to learn the lesson as quickly as possible. However, in the same way that the Bible speaks to God's transforming power, we may indeed learn helpful lessons that shape our Christian character or that help us respond more positively to the pain and suffering of those we encounter. There are many stories of people who have channeled their grief into positive actions, such as setting up scholarships in the name of loved ones who have died or funding research for diseases that they or loved ones have suffered. Others have had their hearts moved in such a way that they dedicate time and resources to alleviating poverty, hunger, and disease. Some work to mediate conflict and bring about reconciliation. These are all good responses to the reality of pain and suffering. I think they suggest something of what God does in response to human ills. These responses seek to transform what has been painful into something meaningful, even beautiful.

Does that mean you must start a foundation or give your money away if you have survived grief or significant illness? Of course not. The examples above are meant to illustrate the way people might respond positively to suffering. In whatever way we respond, our own experiences of suffering should, at the very least, soften our hearts to the experiences of other.

4

What Does the Bible Say about Suffering?

As Christians, the Bible is our primary sourcebook for learning about God. We learn something of the character of God through the stories that have been collected and the way they have been told. We learn about God's love for creation and God's intention to redeem it. We also learn something of the human experience, especially in relationship to God. Throughout the Bible, we are presented with stories of blessing but also stories of suffering.

RESISTING A PROSPERITY GOSPEL

In our time, some Christians choose to focus primarily on stories of blessing. They see them as the pattern for how God relates to those who worship the one true living God. Some people preach or teach that God will bless true believers with all they need to prosper. Blessings, especially material things, are offered as evidence of God's care for God's children and are used to suggest that people are living in right ways. Some people preach and teach that if you simply have enough faith, God will take care of you in abundant fashion.

This so-called **prosperity gospel** tends to focus on the things that make life physically comfortable. If you have much, then you must be living a God-pleasing life. If you have little or are suffering ill health, then you are understood to be out of sync with God's plan for your life. Or perhaps you are being tested and simply need to show more faith so that blessings will shower down. Of course, thinking in this way makes people ill-prepared for losses of any kind. It may even make them doubt their own relationship with God if they don't experience physical blessings.

The Jesus way challenges this kind of thinking. When we look at Jesus' teaching and the way he lived, we see examples of faithfulness that focus on spiritual well-being, not physical well-being. Jesus said that those who want to save their lives will lose them, and that losing one's life is the way to save it (see, for example, Matthew 16:25, Mark 8:35 or John 12:25). In this, Jesus himself serves as our example, giving up his life for ours.

Yet Jesus didn't ignore people's physical condition. The gospel accounts offer many stories of Jesus' willingness to help those who suffered physically. He healed the blind and the lame and those sick with leprosy, and he healed the bleeding woman (see, for example, Matthew 9:27-30; John 5; Mark 1:40-45; Luke 8:42-48). Illnesses of many kinds excluded people from close contact with others. The Jewish rituals connected to purity meant that sick people were often considered unclean. People who were blind or lame were often reduced to begging unless they had family who would support them. In healing them, Jesus wasn't offering wealth and status. In each of these instances, Jesus' healing touch restored the afflicted to full participation in the life of their community.

The experience of Christians throughout history also challenges a prosperity gospel mindset. The apostles were faithful followers of Jesus, and their stories suggest that faithful Christians might expect to suffer in this world. The apostle Paul, for example, experienced all sorts of hardships in his missionary journeys and, like many of the apostles, was likely martyred for his faith. Many of the early missionary apostles experienced great hardship. They were beaten and chased out of town. Many lost their lives because of their faithfulness to Jesus.

The earliest Christians suffered as well, especially for their insistence on worshiping God alone. Some lived with the threat of persecution, while others were arrested and eventually put to death in horrific fashion. They did not aspire to a life of ease, but of faithfulness. Throughout the history of the church there have been episodes of persecution directed at those seeking to preach the gospel or even to simply follow the Jesus way of life. This way has often meant giving up physical prosperity for something far more valuable. As Jesus advises in the Sermon on the Mount, it is better to lay up spiritual treasure than physical treasure! (Matthew 6:19-20).

It seems right to be grateful to God for health and physical provisions. The food and resources we enjoy are rightly acknowledged as evidence of God's care and God's desire for the flourishing of humanity. Acknowledging them as gifts of God reminds us that we are not self-sufficient but are dependent on the God who sustains all of creation.

We must be careful, however, not to think we have these things because we are especially faithful to God. If we take seriously the idea of God's love for all of humankind, then surely Christians who live in places where food isn't abundant or healthcare plentiful are also seeking to be faithful and are finding God near. We know that access to the world's material resources is not distributed fairly across the nations and among various people groups. It seems more honest to view this as the result of human decisions that have concentrated the benefits of resources in patterns that serve the powerful than to see this as God's design for humanity. Furthermore, the Bible is clear in its reminder that from those who have much, much will be expected (Luke 12:48).

If we are honest, we must also admit that being rich in material things or enjoying good health and family relationships isn't limited to those who call themselves Christians. Even the wicked prosper. Do we see that as evidence of God's particular blessing on the way they live their lives? Surely not.

THE SUFFERING OF GOD'S PEOPLE

The Jesus way encourages us to read the Bible differently. In doing so, we begin to realize that God's people have frequently experienced suffering. Sometimes that suffering has grown out of their own sinful rebellions against God and the decisions they made. For example, the Israelites begged God for a king so they could be like other nations, and even though God offered a warning, a king was anointed. Over the generations, Israel suffered the consequences, sometimes living in prosperity but sometimes living under heavy taxation and subject to the suffering brought about by war with the enemies of their kings. In that sense, they were punished for their choices.

In reading these Old Testament stories of conflict and disappointment, we also see how God worked to sustain the people and to bring about their freedom. The chief example of this is the story of the exodus from slavery in Egypt. Through a series of miracles, God's people were set free after many years of oppression by Egyptian leaders. This experience shaped the Hebrew people's understanding of God as a liberating God. Since then, people experiencing oppression and even slavery have looked to God for liberation, seeing in this story evidence of God's preferential care for the vulnerable. Those of us with ample resources should note these stories and God's care for the lowly as well.

SONGS OF LAMENT

It is reassuring to note that in the Bible, God's people are not afraid to express their grief and sorrow. These **laments**, directed toward God, are found in many passages of Scripture. One of the very meaningful resources is the collection of songs known as the psalms of lament.[1] These psalms express the deep frustration of people caught in political strife and dealing with the fear that God has abandoned them. In them, the people plead with God to remember the promises made and the relationship established with their ancestors. They describe suffering in poetic detail and ask, "How long?" (Psalm 79:5). "Show us your steadfast love, O Lord, and grant us your salvation," they plead (85:7).

The communal songs are joined by individual psalms of lament.[2] In these psalms we hear the writers calling out to God for help. They, too, describe the troubles they are experiencing in language that often echoes our own woes. Significantly, they not only look to God for help but express confidence in God's ability and desire to help. In their distress, they often seem to blame God for their woes, but time and again they return to the themes that run throughout Scripture: God is good, God is faithful, God hears and cares for God's people. These laments offer us language and ways to express our own fears and frustrations when we suffer. Generations of believers have taken refuge in these ancient songs, finding comfort in the shared experience of suffering and the hope of relief.

THE STORY OF JOB

Another familiar story in the Bible offers us a way to explore the questions of suffering that have occupied God's people for generations. In the Old Testament story of Job, we meet a very rich man blessed with children and great resources. Job was a devout person of faith who sought to live a blameless life. The story begins with a conversation between God and Satan. In it, God brags about Job, pointing him out as an example of faithful living. Satan tells God that Job is only faithful because his life is easy. If he lost it all, Satan argues, Job would turn and curse God. The storyteller says that God believes Job's faith is genuine, so he allows Satan to interfere in Job's life. Anything is up for grabs, God says, except his own life. As the story unfolds, Job loses his children, his livelihood, and much of what he has accumulated throughout his life. Still, he does not curse God.

Sometimes, this part of the story of Job troubles people. It seems wrong, from our perspective, for God to let Satan inflict Job with so much suffering. Surely a good and just God would care more about Job's family members, his servants, and the flocks that were taken from him, than about proving a point to Satan. What could justify so much suffering on the part of innocent people? This is a valid concern, but not one that the story fully explores. Rather, the focus is on a series of conversations that take place between Job, his friends, and God. It is in these exchanges that we see the writer, and by extension the reader, wrestle with the questions that arise from

Job's suffering as Job voices the grief and concerns of all those who suffer. His "why?" is our question too.

Job's pain is real, and his lament, offered throughout the book, echoes anything we might offer in our own moments of suffering. In the framework of the story, Job's wife and friends ask the same human questions we ask and offer some of the advice and answers we are prone to offer when faced with suffering. Job's wife tells him to curse God and die, but Job refuses, reminding her that if we are willing to accept the good things in life, then we must also accept the difficult (Job 2:9-10). One of his friends suggests that no one who is truly innocent has such trouble in life, so Job must have sin in his life for which he is being punished (Job 4). Another friend insists that if Job turns and pleads with God, his fortunes will be restored. A third friend insists that Job is wrong when Job claims he has not sinned. And when Job pleads his case before God, one friend chastises him for even approaching God with his complaints.

Throughout the long back-and-forth with his friends, Job expresses faith in the ultimate goodness of God even while expressing his own frustration with the suffering he is enduring. His words become our song of praise: "For I know that my Redeemer lives, and that at the last he will stand upon the earth" (Job 19:25).

Part of what is so powerful about Job's story is the honesty of Job's responses. When his friends suggest that the guilty are always punished, Job says, in essence, "Look around! That isn't true. Sometimes the guilty get away with their misdeeds. Those who are evil also live to old age and amass power and property" (see Job 21). Like us, Job pleads with God for answers, frustrated by God's seeming silence in the face of Job's ills.

And finally, God speaks. "Where were you when I laid the foundation of the earth?" he asks (Job 38:4). In other words, who are you to question my ways? Can you do what I can do, create a world and bring it to life? Can you make anything in the natural world happen? And in response, Job humbles himself and admits that he spoke of what he did not know.

Job's questions and observations about the world echo our own, and like Job, we are left with the mystery of God's ways. Job's choices are our choices. Will we insist on staying faithful to God, or will we curse God and die? Can we live with the mystery of God and affirm the hope that one day, God will make all things right? When sitting with the sorrowing, will we be like Job's friends who insist that he find the unconfessed sin? Surely not!

While it may not be all that we want by way of explanation, at some point we must choose how to respond in the face of suffering. We may accept the mystery of God's ways and the reality of a broken world in which sin and evil are still at work while continuing to proclaim trust in God's goodness, or we may curse God and abandon hope in God's ultimate justice.

If we choose to have hope in God's ultimate redemption, we join the community of God's people who have long waited for the fulfillment of God's promises to make all things right. And if we are Jesus followers, we see the beginnings of that fulfillment in Jesus' work on the cross.

JESUS, GOD'S SOLUTION FOR SIN

The writers of the New Testament proclaim that in Jesus, God has begun to fulfill the promises made in the Old Testament. The prophetic voices of the Old Testament repeatedly declared that God would someday send a redeemer, a **messiah** who would free the people and establish a new kingdom. Many who heard the promise expected a political leader, some kind of king who would establish a new kingdom. The gospel writers believed something else. They saw the miracles done by Jesus and heard the message of forgiveness of sins, and they began to understand that the promised kingdom was another kind of kingdom. We speak of this as the **kingdom of God**, and sometimes refer to it as an upside-down kingdom in which the lowly are lifted up and the powerful are humbled. At the center of this kingdom is God who reigns in justice.

This is declared in one of the most famous songs of the Bible. When Jesus' mother, Mary, is told she will bear a child, she responds with a song of praise. In it, she affirms the fulfillment of the ancient promise. "He has brought down the powerful from their thrones, and lifted up the lowly," she proclaims; "he has filled the hungry with good things, and sent the rich away empty. He has helped his servant Israel, in remembrance of his mercy, according to the promise he made to our ancestors, to Abraham and to his descendants forever" (Luke 1:52-55).

Christians believe that in Jesus, God is fulfilling that ancient promise. When his own people rejected his message and turned him over to government officials, Jesus accepted their verdict and allowed himself to be put to death. He did not respond with violence but suffered their wrath, their mocking, and the pain of crucifixion. In his experience of death, Jesus became one with us, bearing our sin and experiencing the reality of the human condition in its separation from God.

Fortunately, the Bible gives witness to another reality in the resurrection of Jesus. Christians believe that God demonstrated his power and ability to defeat sin and death when God raised Jesus from the dead. This power, wrote the apostle Paul, continues to be demonstrated in the lives of believers who experience God's presence and goodness.[3] Ultimately, this offers us hope that someday we, too, will experience the defeat of sin and death.

Finally, in the book of Revelation, we read a vision of what will happen when the fullness of God's intentions for humanity and all the cosmos are brought to fruition. The Bible describes a future reality in which God judges righteously, welcoming all who have suffered to new life. In God's presence, the redeemed are fully healed and fully restored to relationship with God. As the Bible puts it, God "will dwell with them; they will be his peoples, and God himself will with be with them; he will wipe every tear from their eyes. Death will be no more; mourning and crying and pain will be no more, for the first things have passed away" (Revelation 21:3-4).

This is the hope offered to all people, and especially to those who suffer.

5

How Do We Live in the Midst of Suffering?

My recent social media feeds have offered story after story of suffering. It is the anniversary of a mass school shooting, a young college student was murdered, a friend's parent was diagnosed with a terminal illness, and a family feels betrayed by a loved one. You probably have your own list of things that are causing you or someone you love much grief. How do we live with such suffering?

THE "WORK" OF PRAYER

In the previous chapter, the psalms of lament were offered as a reminder that God's people have a history of crying out to God in times of trouble. Reading and praying these psalms are one way to identify with the generations of God's people who have gone before us. They refused to give up hope in the goodness and mercy of God and, like children demanding a parent's attention, called out to God for help. These psalms offer us ways to express our grief, our longing for justice, and our hope for relief.

Some people find comfort in writing their own laments, and certainly we are always invited to pour out our sorrows in prayer. Prayer, however, is not magic. We don't control God or the events around us through prayer. Prayer does not "work" in that fashion. Instead, prayer invites us to stay connected with God and encourages us to draw comfort from God's presence and relationship with us.

This is important because sometimes we begin to doubt the goodness or presence of God when we think our prayers aren't being answered. We might question whether we are praying in the most effective way and may seek to find the words or postures that will bring about the things we most desire. We may try to demonstrate in our prayers that we have learned a lesson, fully confessed sin, or humbled ourselves adequately. Sometimes, we simply try to bargain with God, hoping that what we promise will bring about some relief.

While learning lessons, confessing sin, and searching our hearts and attitudes for a right posture before God are all appropriate, getting them "right" isn't the way to make prayer "work." Prayers aren't meant to work in the sense of making something happen. It isn't a matter of getting the words in the right order or making sure we offer praise before petitions. There is no perfect prayer that will bring about the things we most desire.

THE BIBLE AND PRAYER

The Bible gives us examples of prayers, but it doesn't lay out a precise formula for prayer. Of course, we have the prayer we know as the Lord's Prayer, which arose in response to the disciple's request that Jesus teach them to pray (Luke 11:1). That prayer continues to serve as a model for our prayers in its praise of God, its confession of sin, and its request for daily provision and care. Praying in this fashion is good, but it doesn't mean our requests will necessarily be answered in the ways we most long for. God's ways aren't always our ways, and the reality of suffering in a broken world continues. Even so, we are encouraged to pray, confident that God welcomes our prayers and cares about our hurts.

It can be encouraging to recall the stories in the Bible of God's action in response to the prayers of the people. The longings and groanings of Israel under slavery were heard by God, and the people were led out and eventually brought to their own land.[1] Women such as Sarah and Hannah had their longing for children answered (Genesis 21:1-3; 1 Samuel 1:9-28). In the New Testament, believers were encouraged to pray for healing (James 5:13-16). The apostle Peter knelt in prayer before the disciple Dorcas was raised from the dead (Acts 9:36-41). All these things brought glory to God and served as a witness to God's power and might. But not everyone was healed, and relief from slavery came only after a long period of suffering. Many did not live to see their deepest longings fulfilled. This seems to be the reality of our beautiful yet broken world.

When our prayers are not answered in the way we hope, we may be tempted to think that God has simply ignored our requests or disregarded our needs. We may feel that God is absent or at least very distant from us. We may hurt or grieve so deeply that we cannot even form words to pray. The Bible speaks of this kind of deep grief: in Romans, it speaks of creation itself as being held in bondage to decay, and speaks of the groanings of creation, ourselves, and even the Spirit of

God as it intercedes on our behalf (Romans 8:18-27). Longing for healing and renewal, Christians continue to hope in the promise of God to make all things right in the end.

WHY SHOULD WE PRAY?

We pray because doing so reminds us that we are not all-sufficient. Through prayer, we acknowledge our dependence on God. We name our fears and the longings of our heart, confident that God knows us and loves us. Prayer can help shape our own attitudes and actions so that we reaffirm our faith in God and find strength to persevere even in the midst of profound sorrow or suffering. Naming our griefs and acknowledging our helplessness in the midst of suffering can help us turn toward God. In prayer, we remember that God suffers with us through love for creation and in the experience of Jesus' suffering on the cross.

LIVING IN THE MIDST OF SUFFERING

Accepting the reality of suffering offers us various ways to respond. There are, however, different kinds of suffering, and they may call for different responses.

There are some who suffer, as the Bible puts it, "for the sake of the gospel." The apostle Paul spoke of his imprisonment and the persecution he faced because of his witness for Jesus. Throughout the centuries, those seeking to share the good news of Jesus have been run out of town, have sometimes been physically beaten, and have even been put to death. Many accepted this as the price for following Jesus.

Even if we are not persecuted to this extent, perhaps we suffer in other ways because we refuse to cheat or engage in practices that would take advantage of others. Standing in the way of those who seek to harm others or take advantage of them may lead to our own suffering. Perhaps there is the loss of a job or income, or our position in school or some other community.

There may be consequences to our decision to live the Jesus way of life. Jesus' teaching as recorded in Matthew 5–7, often referred to as the Sermon on the Mount, shows us a way of living in the face of persecution that accepts personal suffering and refuses to use violence as a response. Jesus speaks of going the extra mile and turning the other cheek. Those things serve as a posture for Christians that gives witness to living rightly no matter the cost. This is the kind of suffering we bear as a witness to our faith.

THE EXAMPLE OF THE MARTYRS

In choosing to accept this kind of suffering, we stand alongside the many who have suffered for their faith throughout Christian history. Their example serves as a model of response to suffering that arises because of our commitment to following after Jesus. Reading about their lives and their witness may help sustain us when we endure some measure of suffering.

For example, many Christians early in the church's history faced great pressure to give up their devotion to the Jesus way in favor of worshiping the emperor. Their businesses suffered, they were harassed and jailed, and many were even martyred for their faith. While some caved under pressure, many remained faithful, even to the point of death. The witness they left behind gives testimony to their confidence that God would give strength and endurance to remain faithful to the end. Some spoke of the privilege of martyrdom in that God would trust them to be faithful. They show us a way to live even amid great suffering.

During the sixteenth century, our Anabaptist forebears suffered greatly for their desire to follow Jesus and to form genuine Christian communities. Their desire to separate faith from the political realm was especially seen in the practice of **believers baptism** and their refusal to bear arms. Without the protection of princes or other rulers, many were hunted and killed as heretics.

These stories of faithfulness and martyrdom are captured in the stories of the church and especially in the *Martyrs Mirror*. They offer us a model for perseverance amid societal pressure to give up the Jesus way. We may also be encouraged by the witness of Christians around the world who live in places where following Jesus may lead to estrangement from family or others. In some places, becoming known as a Christian may still result in physical or economic suffering and, at times, even death. Especially for those of us in the West, the stories of persecution around the world may encourage us even while we live in political settings where Christians are free to worship and to participate fully in society.

SUFFERING IN A BROKEN WORLD

Not all suffering is because of persecution, however. As has been noted throughout this little book, suffering comes about for many reasons. We suffer because of the actions of others and even ourselves, we suffer because our bodies fail us, and we suffer the loss of loved ones through death or broken relationship. We suffer individually and as communities. We suffer because sin and evil are still at work in our world.

While we seek to be faithful in following Jesus even in the midst of this kind of suffering, our responses may be somewhat different. We may look for ways to alleviate suffering rather than simply bearing it. Seeking ways to reduce human suffering shouldn't be seen as unwillingness to follow the Jesus way. There is no need to seek martyrdom or the experience of suffering, as if that were the best way to show devotion to God. We should be careful not to glorify suffering as if it were a special sign of faithfulness. This is sometimes a temptation for Christians shaped by the Anabaptist tradition. Suffering isn't something necessary for proving our faithfulness to the world or to God.

For example, refusing medication that manages illness or pain isn't necessary in order to identify with the sufferings of Christ, even though remembering Christ's suffering may encourage us when we experience pain. Refusing to acknowledge our pain or to voice our sorrow because of some expectation that Christians ought to "suffer in silence" or submit to abuse isn't helpful or necessary. We don't seek suffering in order to become more Christlike or to build Christian character. At the same time, we acknowledge that enduring suffering may lead to a honing of our character in ways that are honoring to God.

THE CHALLENGE TO LIVE FAITHFULLY

This is a kind of paradox. Suffering may be made meaningful if it draws us close to the One who creates and sustains us, but we aren't called to go looking for suffering as a way of personal growth. There is no guarantee that suffering will result in a more God-pleasing character. Here, too, sin and brokenness may be at work, corrupting our responses so that we become bitter rather than gracious, and distant rather than drawn ever closer to God. Suffering isn't good for suffering's sake. Suffering is a reality of a broken world, and those who follow Jesus look to the promise of a day when their suffering will be ended and we will be fully in the presence of God.

It is important that we understand this difference. Too often, Christians have turned a blind eye to suffering that could have been alleviated because we have seen acceptance or submission as the only proper response to suffering. This is especially evident in the way Christian communities have often dealt with domestic violence: by calling married women, especially, to model submission to God in their submission to their husband's will. Rather than holding abusers accountable and restraining the violence inflicted on spouses and children, the church has sometimes privileged the covenant of marriage over people's safety and well-being, refusing to acknowledge how deeply and painfully that marriage covenant has already been broken.

This is the kind of suffering that calls for intervention when possible. One of the repeated themes in the Bible has to do with God's desire for justice and God's care for the vulnerable. God is described as the "father of orphans and protector of widows," the one who "gives the desolate a home" and who "leads out the prisoners to prosperity" (Psalm 68:5-6). In the gospel accounts of Jesus' life, we see this same care for those who are hungry, shamed, poor, or sick. Jesus is often found with the outcasts of society, healing them, touching them, restoring them to the community. Likewise, the earliest Christian communities were known for their care of the sick and their willingness to take in abandoned children.

When we join in this kind of activity, we demonstrate our willingness to follow in the way of Jesus. We, too, can care for those who hurt and can help those who are sick. From advocacy to the provision of a hot meal, there are as many ways to care for those who suffer as there are ways of suffering.

This is particularly a role for the community of God's people. In sharing resources, Christians may seek to reduce suffering at home and around the world. For example, relief and development agencies feed people, offer medical care, and engage in community activism in support of vulnerable populations. Some congregations sponsor refugees, feed the homeless, or distribute warm clothing as a way to alleviate suffering in their communities. Grief groups, recovery groups, food trains, and prayer ministries are all positive ways that people may become involved in caring for those who hurt.

What we shouldn't do is tell people who are suffering how to feel, how to pray, or how to believe. At best, and if we are invited, we may be allowed to help them use what some call "the language and grammar of faith."[2] If others express a sense of feeling unloved, abandoned, or punished by God, it may be appropriate to remind them of God's love for humanity and God's forgiving nature. It may simply be that we sit quietly and share in their grief. In any situation, however, we want to avoid arguing over the meaning they are giving to their suffering or offering the trite phrases that suggest we know nothing of deep sorrow or suffering.

USING THE LANGUAGE OF FAITH

In our own experiences of physical and emotional suffering, the language and grammar of faith can provide us ways to understand our experiences. Seeing ourselves as deeply cared for by God invites us to continue looking to God for comfort and care. Remembering that we live in a world where sin's destructive force is still at work may help us to understand ourselves as part of a larger story of creation rather than as singled out for pain and suffering. Understanding that the Jesus way sometimes means we live in ways that open us up to exclusion or harassment isn't easy, but remembering that many before us have given witness to God's sustaining presence may help us be firm in our commitments to follow Jesus to the end.

Finally, when we are uncertain about whether God truly knows or cares about our suffering, we may look to the life of Jesus for assurance that, through the incarnation, God fully understands what it is to be human.

Our Christian confession is that in Jesus, God took on human flesh, becoming one with humanity. Jesus was fully human, like us in all ways except for sin. When we read the gospel accounts of his life, we see Jesus' frequent response to those in need. Matthew describes Jesus as having compassion on the crowds that gathered around him "because they were harassed and helpless" (Matthew 9:36). His response was to heal and restore people to full life. When news of the death of his dear friend Lazarus came to Jesus, the Bible tells us that Jesus wept (John 11:35).

Ultimately, we look to the experience of the cross for assurance that God knows what it is to be human and to suffer. From the physical pain of the crucifixion to the emotional suffering of rejection, in Jesus, God knows the suffering inherent in the human condition.

"My God, my God, why have you forsaken me?" Jesus asked (Matthew 27:46). He was quoting Psalm 22, a psalm of lament. His words echo our own when we feel abandoned by God.

God knows and understands the grief of death. In our **trinitarian** understanding of God, we believe that God the Father suffered in the death of his only begotten Son. This means that we do not seek a God who does not know loss. Rather, we seek a God who knows the deepest kind of loss and has determined to end death once and for all.

In celebrating the resurrection of Christ from the grave, we affirm the promise and hope of an ultimate redemption. We look to the day when the message of the prophets is fully lived out so that the blind see, the lame are restored, and sorrow is no more. Come, Lord Jesus, come.

Glossary

believers baptism: The practice of baptism upon confession of faith rather than as an infant. This practice marked sixteenth-century Anabaptists as heretics in western Europe.

deism: A movement that affirms the existence of a divine Creator who does not intervene in the universe. It is especially associated with a seventeenth- and eighteenth-century intellectual movement that emphasized reason and discounted the supernatural.

incarnation: Refers to the Christian belief that in Jesus, God took on human flesh. Christians affirm Jesus as both human and divine.

kingdom of God: A biblical term used to describe the spiritual realm over which God reigns. It is sometimes referred to as the kingdom of heaven. Christians believe that in Jesus, the kingdom of God has broken into our world.

lament: A deep expression of grief or sorrow.

Martyrs Mirror: Also known as *The Bloody Theater*. A collection of martyr stories first published in 1660 in Holland. While it includes stories from the early church, it especially focuses on the experiences of sixteenth-century Anabaptists. An edition produced in 1685 contains illustrations by Jan Luyken and has been especially influential in Mennonite and Amish communities.

messiah: The anointed one. In the Old Testament, prophets used the term to describe the one who would redeem the people of Israel. In the New Testament, followers of Jesus recognized Jesus as God's anointed, sent to save people from sin.

openness of God: A movement arising in the late twentieth century that affirms God's dynamic relationship with humanity even while questioning classic views of God's foreknowledge and exercise of power. Proponents argue that the future is open rather than predetermined by God, but is moving toward God's promise of full redemption.

process thought: A religious and philosophical movement arising in the twentieth century. Process thought emphasizes becoming (as in moving toward potentiality) and self-determination in all things. The future is unknown because it is still unfolding.

prosperity gospel: A belief that God intends physical well-being and financial abundance for all who have enough faith. These things are seen as evidence of God's blessing.

spiritual warfare: The struggle with supernatural agents, especially the demonic.

theodicy: An explanation for the problem of evil that attempts to show how God is not responsible for evil.

Thomism: The religious and philosophical ideas related to the Catholic priest Thomas Aquinas (1225–1274).

trinitarian: Related to the doctrine of the Trinity, which describes God the Father, the Son, and the Holy Spirit as three in one.

Discussion and Reflection Questions

CHAPTER 1

1. What do you find comforting or disturbing about the statement "Everything happens for a reason"? Has this been helpful or hard to understand?

2. Can you identify an experience of meaning-making in response to something that has caused suffering? How has that helped you or a community you are a part of make sense of that experience?

3. Do you agree with the author that not all pain is bad? Why or why not?

4. Technology continues to shape our experience and understanding of the world. How do you respond to stories of suffering in distant places?

CHAPTER 2

1. When people use the phrase "God is in control," what do you think they mean?
2. The author describes several ways of understanding God's activity in the world. Which do you find most helpful? Most troubling?
3. The author refers to "principalities and powers" as active in our world. Do you think these are human forces or spiritual forces? What shapes your understanding of these forces?
4. How is it helpful to think about God as self-limiting? What troubles you about that concept?

CHAPTER 3

1. Can you describe an experience in which people offered you ways to understand your experience of sorrow or suffering? What was most helpful?
2. How do you understand the biblical story of Joseph and his brothers? Do you think God directed the brothers to sell him into slavery?
3. When good happens as a result of something painful, do you believe that justifies the hurt that was done? Is "evil" ever necessary?
4. Is it helpful to look for the lessons we might learn through suffering? Why or why not?
5. Do you think there is a right way to respond to suffering?

CHAPTER 4

1. How do you respond to stories of persecution or even martyrdom?
2. Do you think that following the Jesus way will inevitably lead to suffering?
3. How has reading or praying the psalms offered comfort?
4. In the story of Job, we are presented with the mystery of God's action. Is it wrong for us to seek answers from God?
5. How do you understand Jesus' life, death, and resurrection as offering hope in the midst of suffering?

CHAPTER 5

1. What do you understand the purpose of prayer to be?
2. What do you think it means to suffer persecution for following Jesus? Can you offer examples from your own or others' experience?
3. In the Anabaptist tradition, martyr stories have served as examples of faithful Christian living. In what ways is this helpful? Is it ever unhelpful?
4. Should suffering always be viewed as a way of sharing Christ's suffering?
5. How have you seen the Christian community work to alleviate suffering?
6. Is it enough to know that God suffers with us? Why or why not?

Shared Convictions

Mennonite World Conference, a global community of Christian churches that facilitates community between Anabaptist-related churches, offers these shared convictions that characterize Anabaptist faith. For more on Anabaptism, go to ThirdWay.com.

By the grace of God, we seek to live and proclaim the good news of reconciliation in Jesus Christ. As part of the one body of Christ at all times and places, we hold the following to be central to our belief and practice:

1. God is known to us as Father, Son and Holy Spirit, the Creator who seeks to restore fallen humanity by calling a people to be faithful in fellowship, worship, service and witness.

2. Jesus is the Son of God. Through his life and teachings, his cross and resurrection, he showed us how to be faithful disciples, redeemed the world, and offers eternal life.

3. As a church, we are a community of those whom God's Spirit calls to turn from sin, acknowledge Jesus Christ as Lord, receive baptism upon confession of faith, and follow Christ in life.

4. As a faith community, we accept the Bible as our authority for faith and life, interpreting it together under Holy Spirit guidance, in the light of Jesus Christ to discern God's will for our obedience.

5. The Spirit of Jesus empowers us to trust God in all areas of life so we become peacemakers who renounce violence, love our enemies, seek justice, and share our possessions with those in need.

6. We gather regularly to worship, to celebrate the Lord's Supper, and to hear the Word of God in a spirit of mutual accountability.

7. As a world-wide community of faith and life we transcend boundaries of nationality, race, class, gender and language. We seek to live in the world without conforming to the powers of evil, witnessing to God's grace by serving others, caring for creation, and inviting all people to know Jesus Christ as Saviour and Lord.

In these convictions we draw inspiration from Anabaptist forebears of the 16th century, who modelled radical discipleship to Jesus Christ. We seek to walk in his name by the power of the Holy Spirit, as we confidently await Christ's return and the final fulfillment of God's kingdom.

Adopted by Mennonite World Conference General Council, March 15, 2006

Notes

Introduction

  1 Judith Viorst and Ray Cruz, illustrator, *Alexander and the Terrible, Horrible, No Good, Very Bad Day* (Atheneum Books for Young Readers, 1987).

Chapter 1

  1 Alister E. McGrath, *Christian Theology: An Introduction*, 5th ed. (Chicester, West Sussex: John Wiley and Sons, 2011), 352–53.

  2 Stanley J. Grenz, *Created for Community: Connecting Christian Belief with Christian Living* (Grand Rapids, MI: Baker Academic, 1996).

Chapter 2

  1 Gary Trudeau, *Doonesbury*, October 5, 2001, available at https://www.gocomics.com/doonesbury/2001/10/05.

  2 See Alister McGrath's discussion of divine power in *Christian Theology: An Introduction*, 5th ed. (Chicester, West Sussex: John Wiley and Sons, 2011), 212–15.

Chapter 4

1 Bible scholar Claus Westermann identifies the communal psalms as Psalms 44, 60, 74, 79, 80, 83, 89. See Claus Westermann, *The Psalms: Structure, Content and Message*, trans. Ralph D. Gehrke (Minneapolis: Augsburg Publishing House, 1980), 29.

2 Westermann classifies these as Psalms 3, 4, 5, 6, 7, 9–14, 22–23, 25–28, 31, 35–36, 38–39, 51–59, 61–64, 69, 71, 73, 86, 88, 102, 109, 130, with several others partially included. Ibid., 53.

3 See, for example, Romans 8:11, Ephesians 1:15-23, or the Apostle Peter's message in Acts 2.

Chapter 5

1 The story of release from Egypt and the journey to a land of their own is found in Exodus, Leviticus, Numbers, and Deuteronomy.

2 Jonathan R. Wilson, *Why Church Matters: Worship, Ministry, and Mission in Practice* (Grand Rapids, MI: Brazos Press, 2006), 59–72.

The Author

Valerie G. Rempel serves as dean of Fresno Pacific Biblical Seminary and vice president of Fresno Pacific University in Fresno, California. She has degrees from Tabor College, Mennonite Brethren Biblical Seminary, and Vanderbilt University, and she has served on a variety of Mennonite Brethren and inter-Mennonite boards. Rempel is a member of Willow Avenue Mennonite Church.

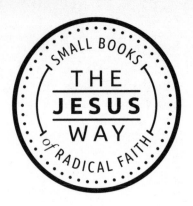

SMALL BOOKS
THE
JESUS
WAY
of RADICAL FAITH

**What Is the Bible and
How Do We Understand It?**

by Dennis R. Edwards

**Why Did Jesus Die and What
Difference Does It Make?**

by Michele Hershberger

**What Is the Trinity
and Why Does It Matter?**

by Steve Dancause

**Why Do We Suffer and
Where Is God When We Do?**

by Valerie G. Rempel

**Who Are Our Enemies and
How Do We Love Them?**

by Hyung Jin Kim Sun

(SUMMER 2020)

**What Is God's Mission in the
World and How Do We Join It?**

by Juan F. Martínez

(FALL 2020)

**What Is the Church
and Why Does It Exist?**

by David Fitch

(FALL 2020)

**What Does Justice
Look Like and Why
Does God Care about It?**

by Judith and Colin McCartney

(FALL 2020)

**What Is God's Kingdom
and What Does
Citizenship Look Like?**

by César García

(SPRING 2021)

**Who Was Jesus and What
Does It Mean to Follow Him?**

by Nancy Elizabeth Bedford

(SPRING 2021)

HERALD
PRESS

www.HeraldPress.com. 1-800-245-7894